But It Hurts to Let Go

THERAPEUTIC WORKBOOK

HOLLEY BROCK

Holley Brock
Assisted by Global Destiny Enterprise, LLC
Cover design by: Angela Mills Camper of Dezign Pro Printing & Graphics
Interior Formatting by C.E. Higgins on Fiverr (carlyhiggins)
Amplified Bible (AMP)
Scripture quotations are taken from the Amplified® Bible (AMP), Copyright © 2015 by The Lockman Foundation. Used by permission.

Printed in the United States of America
First Printing, 2024
ISBN: 979-8-9873254-3-8

But It Hurts To Let Go

THERAPEUTIC
WORKBOOK

UNDERSTANDING THE EFFECTS
OF GRIEF ON THE SOUL.

HOLLEY BROCK

CONTENTS

Introduction

GRIEF HAS NO prejudices or age requirements; it chooses its victims indiscriminately. Grief does not schedule a convenient appointment on your organized calendar, nor does it consider the plans you have made. It comes in like a thief in the night, stealing more than you could ever imagine. Simply put, grief is a thief, taking what you did not even know could be taken. The Bible reminds us in John 10:10, "The thief comes only to steal and kill and destroy. I came that they may have and enjoy life, and have it in abundance [to the full, till it overflows]." Grief is no different; it comes to steal your joy, kill your hope, and destroy your future.

This Therapeutic Workbook is the companion to But It Hurts to Let Go: Understanding the Effects of Grief on the Soul. It is designed to help you identify the areas of your life that have been robbed by loss and grief, guiding you on a journey of self-discovery and healing. Once you have identified the thief, you must decide to stop him from taking anything else and reclaim everything that has been stolen. It is time to get your fight back and see yourself not as a victim but as a victor through Jesus Christ!

1

THE PSYCHOLOGY OF GRIEF

GRIEF 101

Grief is simply the heart's response to trying to find the easiest way to let go (Dr. Hart Ramsey). We know that there is often no easy way of letting go. Grief then becomes the process of dealing with loss. We may experience many different symptoms associated with grief without realizing that it is at the root. We spend much of our lives trying to kill fruit that continues to grow and reproduce because the root cause was never addressed. It is time to identify the root causes of the symptoms you have experienced and are experiencing. Once that is done, you can be assured that the fruit will stop growing. The only fruit we should bear is the fruit of the Spirit!

1. How would you describe your experience with personal grief? How do you experience someone else's grief? What was it like for you to

observe someone you care about grieving?

_____

_____

_____

_____

_____

_____

_____

2. How do you currently process perceived loss? Why? If you struggle with processing how you feel, identify the barriers.

_____

_____

_____

_____

_____

_____

_____

3. Read Jeremiah 17:9. Write what the Holy Spirit reveals to you about the secret motives of your heart.

_____

_____

_____

_____

_____

_____

_____

_____

4. What false narrative(s) have you accepted about grief that is causing deceit in your heart?

_____

_____

_____

_____

_____

_____

_____

5. What somatic symptoms have you experienced due to negative emotions and/or grief?

_____

_____

_____

_____

_____

_____

6. Do you place more significance on the actual loss itself or do you find yourself consumed with the feelings and emotions associated with grief?

_____

_____

_____

_____

_____

_____

_____

7. Do you experience feelings of guilt? What do you feel guilty about? What would you have done differently if given the opportunity?

_____

_____

_____

_____

_____

_____

_____

_____

_____

_____

THE TRAUMA OF GRIEF

1. Have you experienced a traumatic loss? What happened? What came up as you thought about it?

_____

_____

_____

_____

_____

_____

_____

2. Now that you understand Post Traumatic Stress Disorder, do you feel that grief may have been delayed due to experiencing PTSD? Explain.

_____

_____

_____

_____

_____

_____

_____

_____

_____

GRIEF AND THE BRAIN

1. How has grief affected your ability to concentrate and remember important things?

_____

_____

_____

_____

_____

_____

_____

2. Is your mood dysregulated due to grief? How has your mood been recently?

_____

_____

_____

_____

_____

_____

_____

_____

_____

3. How has grief disrupted your sleep?

_____

_____

_____

_____

_____

_____

_____

4. Do you find yourself ruminating about the event or person that has caused you to experience grief? Have you been thinking about how different things could have been? What thoughts occupy your mind?

_____

_____

_____

_____

_____

_____

_____

_____

_____

_____

5. What social support do you have in your grieving process? What support do you feel is missing? What are the barriers to receiving the social support you may need?

_____

_____

_____

_____

_____

_____

_____

2

LIFE IS LIKE A BOX OF CHOCOLATES

THE STAGES OF GRIEF

In this chapter, we explore the unpredictability of life and the various stages we may encounter. As we go through life, we will always find ourselves either entering or exiting a stage. The same is true for the different seasons in our lives. Ecclesiastes 3:1-4 reminds us that there is a timeline for everything. We are often frustrated with ourselves and God when His timeline does not align with ours. We cannot avoid the process, nor do we have the option to skip certain stages.

1. How do you typically handle situations that you have no control over? Do you respond in frustration or anger?

_____

_____

_____

_____

_____

_____

_____

_____

_____

2. Do you trust that God is in control of your life and that He is aware of every present circumstance? Why? Why not?

_____

_____

_____

_____

_____

_____

_____

3. How would you describe the current state of your life?

_____

_____

_____

_____

_____

_____

_____

_____

_____

DENIAL

Denial is considered the initial stage of grief. However, as previously stated, it does not mean it is the first stage a grieving person may experience. In the field of psychology, denial is defined as the conscious refusal to perceive that painful facts exist.

1. Look up the word "denial" in the dictionary and write down its synonyms. Are there any synonyms that resonate with you? Why? What resonated with you about those words?

_____

_____

_____

_____

_____

_____

_____

2. Has anyone told you that you are in a state of denial? How did you feel hearing this about yourself?

_____

_____

_____

_____

_____

_____

_____

_____

3. Do you feel that you are in denial about the situation that has caused you grief? Why? Why not? Explain.

_____

_____

_____

_____

_____

_____

_____

4. How has denial prolonged your healing process?

_____

_____

_____

_____

_____

_____

_____

_____

5. In terms of relationships (friendship and/or romantic) has it been difficult for you to move forward because you are in denial that it ended? What are you in denial about? Is it your memories? Is it your feelings? Is it not having closure?

_____

_____

_____

_____

_____

_____

_____

6. Read Galatians 5:17. How has your refusal to deny the flesh contributed to your grief? In what areas do you need to deny the flesh? In what areas do you need to feed your spirit?

_____

_____

_____

_____

_____

_____

_____

_____

_____

ANGER

Anger is a universal emotion, which means regardless of race, culture, language, or even the country it is expressed in, you know when someone is angry. We tend to categorize our level of anger by being "mad or Big Mad."

1. How do you express anger? How do you cope when you are angry? Are your coping skills healthy or unhealthy? How might you improve your coping skills?

_____

_____

_____

_____

_____

_____

_____

_____

_____

_____

2. Anger is a secondary emotion and a cover-up for other emotions. What emotions do you feel anger is concealing—fear, loss, or sadness?

_____

_____

_____

_____

_____

_____

_____

3. When a person experiences loss, the natural reaction is to fight for what was lost, to take flight from the situation altogether, or to remain frozen in fear. How are you responding to loss—fight, flight, freeze?

_____

_____

_____

_____

_____

_____

_____

_____

4. Is your anger the result of not having control? What *do* you have control of?

_____

_____

_____

_____

_____

_____

_____

5. Are you angry at yourself? Are you angry at others? Are you angry at God? Ask the Holy Spirit to guide your heart in response to these questions.

_____

_____

_____

_____

_____

_____

_____

_____

_____

BARGAINING

Merriam-Webster dictionary defines the word "bargaining" as, "an agreement between parties settling what each one gives or receives in a transaction between them or what course of action or policy each pursues in respect to the other."

1. Have you tried to make deals, or bargain with God concerning the loss? Write the details of the bargain.

_____

_____

_____

_____

_____

_____

2. Read Psalm 119 (in its entirety). Write out the verses that minister to you.

_____

_____

_____

_____

_____

_____

_____

_____

_____

_____

3. Are you currently experiencing feelings of guilt or self-blame? Why?

_____

_____

_____

_____

_____

_____

_____

4. In what other ways have you used bargaining to regain control?

_____

_____

_____

_____

_____

_____

_____

DEPRESSION

Depression is simply defined as extreme sadness or despair.

1. Look up scriptures about sadness and despair. Write down 2-3 of them.

_____

_____

_____

_____

_____

_____

2. What physical symptoms have you experienced due to depression?

_____

_____

_____

_____

_____

_____

_____

3. What emotional symptoms have you experienced due to depression?

_____

_____

_____

_____

_____

_____

_____

4. Has your grief been so prolonged that it has become a spirit of grief? What soul wound is at the root of your grief?

_____

_____

_____

_____

_____

_____

5. How have you dealt with the emotional pain of your grief? How do you process feelings of sadness?

_____

_____

_____

_____

_____

_____

_____

_____

ACCEPTANCE

According to Kübler-Ross, acceptance is considered the final stage in the grieving process. We define this stage as a possible experience that signifies one has come to a resolution in the grief process.

1. Do you feel that you have reached the acceptance stage of grief? How do you know? Are there barriers preventing you from reaching acceptance?

_____

_____

_____

_____

_____

_____

_____

_____

2. Look up synonyms for the word "acceptance." Write down the words that stand out to you.

_____

_____

_____

_____

_____

_____

_____

_____

3. Have you accepted the will of God for your life? What about God's will for others?

_____

_____

_____

_____

_____

_____

_____

_____

4. How have immaturity, selfishness, disobedience, and impatience created a loss in your life?

_____

_____

_____

_____

_____

_____

_____

5. Have you found peace of mind concerning the loss? Look up Bible verses about peace and write them down.

_____

_____

_____

_____

_____

_____

_____

_____

_____

MEANING AND GROWTH

1. Have you been able to see the goodness of God during your loss? How has He shown Himself to be good?

_____

_____

_____

_____

_____

_____

_____

_____

_____

2. Read Romans 8:27-28. In your own words, write down what this scripture means.

_____

_____

_____

_____

_____

_____

_____

_____

3. Do you struggle with believing that God loves you? Why?

_____

_____

_____

_____

_____

_____

_____

_____

_____

4. What physical changes do you desire? Are they emotional, mental, social, or spiritual?

_____

_____

_____

_____

_____

_____

_____

_____

_____

5. In what ways have you grown because of loss? What lessons did loss teach you?

_____

_____

_____

_____

_____

_____

_____

_____

_____

_____

_____

_____

_____

_____

_____

_____

3
WHEN LOSS BECOMES GRIEF

NOT SO GOOD GRIEF

The word "loss" can be defined in various ways: destruction or ruin; the act or fact of being unable to keep or maintain something or someone; the partial or complete deterioration or absence of a physical capability or function; the harm or privation resulting from losing or being separated from someone or something; an instance of losing someone or something; failure to gain, win, obtain, or utilize.

1. Read the above definitions again. Which definition of loss do you feel accurately describes your current loss? Describe what the loss is.

_____

_____

_____

_____

_____

_____

_____

_____

2. When you think about the loss, did you experience feelings of grief first and then discover your heart was processing a loss? Or did you suffer the loss first and then subsequent grief? Explain.

_____

_____

_____

_____

_____

_____

_____

3. What situations in your life were "hard" losses? What was it? How did you process it? Are you still experiencing grief because of it?

_____

_____

_____

_____

_____

DELAYED GRIEF

Delay can be defined as the act of postponing, hindering, or causing something to occur more slowly than normal; the state of being; to stop, detain, or hinder for a time.

1. Have you experienced a delayed response to a loss? How did you know the grief was delayed?

_____

_____

_____

_____

_____

_____

_____

2. "The heart takes longer to process what the mind already knows." What does this statement mean to you?

_____

_____

_____

_____

_____

_____

_____

3. Have you ever had something good happen in your life, yet you experienced grief because it was also accompanied by loss?

_____

_____

_____

_____

_____

_____

_____

4. When you realized that you were experiencing delayed grief, did you allow yourself to process the emotions, or did you attempt to suppress them? Why?

_____

_____

_____

_____

_____

_____

_____

GRIEF BEFORE LOSS

For all who are allowing themselves to be led by the Spirit of God are sons of God. For you have not received a spirit of slavery leading again to fear [of God's judgment], but you have received the Spirit of adoption as sons [the Spirit producing sonship] by which we [joyfully] cry, "Abba! Father!" The Spirit Himself testifies and confirms together with our spirit [assuring us] that we [believers] are children of God. And if [we are His] children, [then we are His] heirs also: heirs of God and fellow heirs with Christ [sharing His spiritual blessing and inheritance], if indeed we share in His suffering so that we may also share in His glory. (Romans 8:14-18)

1. What does the above scripture mean to you as it relates to being led by the spirit? Explain.

_____

_____

_____

_____

_____

_____

_____

_____

_____

2. Have you ever experienced an overwhelming sense of grief but were unable to pinpoint what the root cause was? What did you sense? How did you feel?

_____

_____

_____

_____

_____

_____

_____

3. Read Isaiah 43:18-19. Discuss how a season of transition was also a season of perceived loss and grief. What was the situation? What were you grieving?

_____

_____

_____

_____

_____

_____

_____

_____

4. How have you missed clues given by the Holy Spirit that transition was on the horizon?

_____

_____

_____

_____

_____

_____

_____

_____

PRE-GRIEF

When we experience grief as the initial phase of transition, our responsibility is to seek God about what is on the horizon for our lives. It is then that our prayer should be, "Lord, not my will, but Your will be done."

1. Is it challenging for you to align your will with the will of God? Why? What is challenging? How do you respond to God's will?

_____

_____

_____

_____

_____

_____

_____

_____

_____

2. What does it mean for God to be the Author and Finisher of your faith? (Hebrews 12:2). How does this relate to loss?

_____

_____

_____

_____

_____

_____

_____

_____

_____

_____

_____

_____

4
MISERY LOVES COMPANY

EMPATHY VS. SYMPATHY

It is human nature to feel empathy and sympathy for the sufferings of mankind.

Study *2 Corinthians 1:3-4:*

> *Blessed [gratefully praised and adored] be the God and Father of our Lord Jesus Christ, the Father of mercies and the God of all comfort, who comforts and encourages us in every trouble so that we will be able to comfort and encourage those who are in any kind of trouble, with the comfort with which we ourselves are comforted by God.*

1. Do you struggle with being empathetic or sympathetic toward others? Why?

_____

_____

_____

_____

_____

_____

_____

_____

_____

_____

2. Does it cause discomfort when others are empathetic or sympathetic toward you? Why? How do you respond?

_____

_____

_____

_____

_____

_____

_____

_____

3. Have others misunderstood your suffering? How? Have you misunderstood the suffering of others? Explain.

_____

_____

_____

_____

_____

_____

_____

_____

_____

4. How did you feel when someone said they "know what you are going through" concerning a loss? Did you feel dismissed or insignificant?

_____

_____

_____

_____

_____

_____

_____

SHARED GRIEF

Shared grief refers to the collective experience of mourning or sorrow felt by a group of people such as a family, community, or society, following a significant loss or tragedy. It's a shared emotional response to a common loss that affects multiple individuals or a community.

1. Have you experienced a loss where grief was shared? What was the loss? With what group was the grief shared?

_____

_____

_____

_____

_____

_____

_____

2. Has a loss been difficult to process because of the intense shared grief of others? How has the grief of others affected you?

_____

_____

_____

_____

_____

_____

_____

3. Has the happiness of others ever caused you to experience other positive emotions? What was the situation? How did you feel?

_____

_____

_____

_____

_____

_____

_____

4. How has having the support of others who are sharing in your grief brought you comfort? How has not having the support of others prolonged grief?

_____

_____

_____

_____

_____

_____

_____

MISERY LOVES COMPANY

1. What does "Misery loves company" mean to you?

_____

_____

_____

_____

_____

_____

_____

2. Have people you were close to made a mockery of your pain? How? Did you respond? Why? Why not?

_____

_____

_____

_____

_____

_____

_____

3. When you are experiencing emotional pain, do you seek others who are also hurting because you feel they "get it"? Why? Why not?

_____

_____

_____

_____

_____

_____

4. Read 1 Peter 5:7. Write about how you will cast your cares on Jesus.

_____

_____

_____

_____

_____

_____

_____

5

I GRIEVE. YOU GRIEVE. WE ALL GRIEVE

JUST LIVE LONG ENOUGH

It is funny how when you are younger, the things your parents and grandparents talked about seem so foreign and old-fashioned. The stories they shared with you about their experiences were far away from anything that you could imagine for your life. Then one day, you realize their stories make sense because you have lived long enough to have your own similar experiences.

1. What advice were you given when you were younger that now makes sense as an adult because you lived through it?

_____

_____

_____

_____

_____

_____

_____

_____

2. Did the loss in your life catch you off guard like a thief in the night? How? Do you think it would have been different had you been able to prepare yourself for the loss? Explain.

_____

_____

_____

_____

_____

_____

_____

3. When you look at your life, what has grief cost you? What has grief taken from you?

_____

_____

_____

_____

_____

_____

_____

_____

_____

_____

4. In this exercise, you will write a letter to grief. In the letter: (a) identify where you were or what you were doing when grief showed up, (b) discuss how the grief makes you feel, (c) detail the areas in your life that have been contaminated by grief, (d) close the letter with a farewell to the grief, commanding it to leave your life.

_____

_____

_____

_____

_____

_____

_____

_____

_____

_____

_____

_____

_____

PREPARING FOR GRIEF

1. Growing up, were there conversations about loss and grief? If yes, how did these conversations prepare you as an adult for loss? If not, what do you wish you had been told about loss and grief?

_____

_____

_____

_____

_____

_____

_____

2. What is your earliest memory of death? Who died? How did you feel? Did you have comfort and support? If yes, what did that support look like? If not, what do you feel you needed at that time you did not have?

_____

_____

_____

_____

_____

_____

_____

3. Are there unhealed areas of your heart that still hurt because you did not process the loss properly or perhaps not at all? What loss still causes you pain?

_____

_____

_____

_____

_____

_____

_____

_____

Exercise: Lay your hand over your heart and talk to God about what you are feeling. Write down what He says to you.

KNOW BETTER, DO BETTER

1. How have you suffered in silence due to grief? Who or what silenced you?

_____

_____

_____

_____

_____

_____

_____

_____

_____

2. Is grief currently taboo in your family? Is there a community within your family to process loss and grief? What does it look like? How can you create an environment of emotional transparency and vulnerability in your family or friends?

_____

_____

_____

_____

_____

_____

_____

3. Is it important for you to check on others who have experienced loss? How do you check on them? Describe the type of support you need from others when you are experiencing emotional pain. What do people say or do that causes you to feel worse? How do you provide support for yourself when hurting? Do you pray, worship, or engage in social activities?

_____

_____

_____

6

BUT IT HURTS

UNHEALED WOUNDS

Emotional pain can be debilitating. It can scream from the depths of your innermost being and completely shake you to your core. It can be the invisible prison that seeks to keep you bound. Unresolved emotional pain creates unhealed wounds.

1. Merriam-Webster defines debilitating as: "causing serious impairment of strength or ability to function." What areas of your life have been debilitated by grief? Look up scriptures that strengthen your spirit.

_____

_____

_____

_____

_____

_____

_____

_____

2. In what ways has loss changed the course of your life? Explain.

_____

_____

_____

_____

_____

_____

_____

3. Read Jeremiah 29:11. Write what this scripture means in your own words. Does this scripture give you peace knowing that God has plans to give you hope and a future, even amid grief? How so?

_____

_____

_____

_____

_____

_____

4. Read Psalm 34 in its entirety. Write down every instruction that David gives and every promise from God.

_____

_____

_____

_____

_____

_____

_____

_____

_____

_____

_____

_____

_____

_____

_____

5. Have you suppressed your own emotional pain because you felt someone else's pain was more important? Did someone cause you to feel that way or was it a narrative you created yourself? Explain.

_____

_____

_____

_____

_____

_____

_____

_____

HIDDEN PAIN

1. In what ways have you attempted to hide your pain from others? Who did you try to hide from? Do you feel you were successful? Why or why not? Why did you feel the need to hide your feelings from others?

_____

_____

_____

_____

_____

_____

_____

2. In what ways has unresolved emotional pain contaminated those closest to you?

_____

_____

_____

_____

_____

_____

_____

_____

3. Have you reacted inappropriately to someone because they unknowingly bumped into a tender area of woundedness? What did they say/do? How did you react? What would you do differently?

_____

_____

_____

_____

_____

_____

_____

_____

GRIEF IS CONTAGIOUS

1. Have you had a loss that created a mix of emotions such as anger and sadness or relief and guilt? Describe the situation and the conflicting emotions.

_____

_____

_____

_____

_____

_____

_____

_____

2. Sometimes we may feel having emotional wounds is a sign of weakness. Why do you think you have to be the superhero in your own story?

_____

_____

_____

_____

_____

_____

_____

_____

_____

_____

3. Read 2 Corinthians 12:9-11:

> But He has said to me, "My grace is sufficient for you [My
> lovingkindness and My mercy are more than enough—always
> available—regardless of the situation]; for [My] power is being
> perfected [and is completed and shows itself most
> effectively] in [your] weakness." Therefore, I will all the more
> gladly boast in my weaknesses, so that the power of Christ [may

completely enfold me and] may dwell in me. 10 So I am well pleased with weaknesses, with insults, with distresses, with persecutions, and with difficulties, for the sake of Christ; for when I am weak [in human strength], then I am strong [truly able, truly powerful, truly drawing from God's strength].

Exercise: After reading 2 Corinthians 12:9-11, how do you find strength in God through your weakness?

_____

_____

_____

_____

_____

_____

_____

_____

4. Is it okay for you not to be okay? What is challenging for you about not being okay? Explain.

_____

_____

_____

_____

_____

_____

NUMBING THE PAIN

It is human nature to move away from pain and toward pleasure.

1. What does "numbing the pain" mean?

_____

_____

_____

_____

_____

_____

_____

2. Have you ever attempted to medicate your pain? How? Are you currently medicating your pain? What were the consequences? Do you know someone who medicates their pain? What would your advice be to them?

_____

_____

_____

_____

_____

_____

_____

_____

_____

3. Are you an emotional eater? Do you eat your emotions? What are the consequences? Or do you restrict food when experiencing emotional pain? Do you know someone who eats their emotions? What would your advice be to them?

_____

_____

_____

_____

_____

_____

_____

_____

4. Have you attempted to numb your pain through fornication/sex? How did you feel after making that decision? What were the consequences? Do you know someone who sexually acts out when they are hurting? What advice would you give them?

_____

_____

_____

_____

_____

_____

_____

_____

5. What thirst has your emotional pain created that you have not allowed Jesus to quench? Why?

Exercise: Write a prayer of repentance to God for improper and illegal methods used to numb the pain.

_____

_____

_____

_____

_____

_____

_____

_____

_____

_____

_____

_____

_____

Write a letter of forgiveness to yourself for the choices you made to feel anything other than the pain.

_____

_____

_____

_____

_____

_____

_____

_____

_____

_____

_____

_____

_____

_____

_____

_____

7
SITUATIONAL AWARENESS

UNEXPECTED GRIEF

Situational awareness refers to the ability to perceive and understand what is happening around you, to comprehend the meaning of those events, and to predict how they will affect you in the near future. It involves being aware of the environment, recognizing potential threats or changes, and making informed decisions based on that information.

Key components of situational awareness include:

· *Perception:* Noticing and identifying relevant information in the environment.

· *Comprehension:* Understanding what the perceived information means in context.

· *Projection:* Anticipating future states and developments based on the current situation.

1. On a scale from 1-10, rate your overall level of situational awareness. Why did you rate yourself the way you did? How perceptive

are you? How well do you comprehend? Do you do well with projecting? Explain.

_____

_____

_____

_____

_____

_____

_____

_____

_____

2. "Discernment" is defined as the ability to judge well. How would you rate your level of discernment? What is hindering your ability to judge well? How might you improve your discernment?

_____

_____

_____

_____

_____

_____

3. How do you know something is going on in your soul and spirit? How do you respond to this?

_____

_____

_____

_____

_____

_____

UNKNOWN GRIEF

1. Have you ever experienced pain in your soul but could not identify its source? What emotions were you experiencing? How did you reconcile what you sensed but did not know?

_____

_____

_____

_____

_____

_____

2. Do you remember the first time someone broke your heart? What was the situation? Have you ever broken your own heart? How? Has there been a time when you felt that God broke your heart? What happened?

Exercise: Write a letter to each person (including yourself and God) that broke your heart, releasing them into your forgiveness.

_____

_____

_____

_____

_____

_____

_____

_____

_____

_____

_____

_____

_____

_____

PEOPLE

1. Has a loss been challenging because you had a soul tie? How did you know you had a soul tie? If you are not sure what a soul tie is, do a biblical study on soul ties and write down what you learned.

_____

_____

_____

_____

_____

_____

_____

_____

2. One of the hardest and most painful lessons to grow through is when God is taking you somewhere that your friends cannot go. Have you had to let go of a friend due to what God instructed you to do? Who was it? How did you move forward without the person? How did you feel then? How do you feel now?

Exercise: Write a letter to the friend who is no longer walking with you into your future. Tell your friend why it was necessary and what you hope for their future.

_____

_____

_____

_____

_____

_____

_____

_____

_____

_____

_____

_____

_____

3. Have you lost a friend whom God called home? Who was it? What happened? How did you move forward without your friend? How did you feel then? How do you feel now?

Exercise: Write a letter to the friend who is resting in the arms of Jesus. Tell them about how life has been without them. If you are angry at your friend for leaving you, express how you feel but also offer your forgiveness.

_____

_____

_____

_____

_____

_____

_____

4. Have you lost a parent through death or a severed relationship? Who was it? What happened? How did you feel then? How do you feel now? Do you have closure? Why? Why not?

Exercise: Write a letter to the parent who is no longer in your life. Let them know how your life has been impacted by their absence. What did you need from them? If you are angry at your parent for not being in your life, offer them your forgiveness and honor.

_____

_____

_____

_____

_____

_____

_____

_____

_____

_____

_____

5. Have you had to bury a child (this includes adult children) or a close sibling? Who was it? What happened? How did you feel about it then? How do you feel about it now? (Include grief that may be related to an abortion).

Exercise: Write a letter to the child or sibling who is resting in the arms of Jesus. Let them know how your life has been impacted by their departure.

What do you miss about them? If you are angry at them for not being in your life, offer them your forgiveness. If you had an abortion, repent for the innocent blood shed and ask God to heal that broken place in your heart.

_____

_____

_____

_____

_____

_____

_____

_____

_____

_____

_____

_____

6. Have you ever behaved out of character because someone you loved betrayed or hurt you? What was the situation? Who was involved? What did you do? How do you feel about it now when you look back on it? What would you have done differently (if anything)?

_____

_____

_____

_____

_____

_____

7. Have you experienced the grief of divorce? What was the situation? What was the most challenging thing to process? What emotions still come up when you think about it? If you are still angry, write down what you are angry about and offer them your forgiveness. Forgiveness is for you, not for the other person.

_____

_____

_____

_____

_____

_____

_____

PLACES

Transition may include moving from one side of town to another, moving to a new city, or even possibly relocating to a different state.

Discuss a transition you experienced that caused a sense of loss and grief. What was the situation? How did you feel? Are transitions still challenging for you? Why?

_____

_____

_____

_____

_____

_____

_____

_____

_____

_____

_____

_____

2. Do you have a connection to a certain place that whenever you leave creates sadness? What is the place? What is the connection? Is it the people? Is it the memories? Explain.

_____

_____

_____

_____

_____

_____

_____

_____

THINGS

1. Are there "things" you have lost or had to let go of that have been a source of grief? What are the things? What was the situation that required you to let go? Are there things that you are still holding on to because the thought of letting them go is too painful? What are they? Why is letting them go challenging?

_____

_____

_____

_____

_____

_____

_____

2. Read Job 1:21. Write what this scripture means to you and how it applies to your own life.

_____

_____

_____

_____

_____

8

NOT WHO I WAS

LOSS OF IDENTITY

We go through many different seasons in life where we may feel that we have lost ourselves. There are other seasons when we feel as though God has lost us.

1. Have you ever felt that God got it wrong concerning your kingdom identity? (For example, He has called you to be a minister but everything in you disagrees or maybe your life is contrary to what He is calling you to be.) Why is it challenging for you to accept your kingdom identity? Do you grieve who you used to be? Why?

_____

_____

_____

_____

_____

_____

_____

_____

_____

2. Do you know who you are in the kingdom? Do others know? If you do not know, spend some time in prayer asking the Holy Spirit who you are in God's eyes. Write down what He reveals to you. If others do not know, ask yourself why they are unaware. Write down your reasoning.

_____

_____

_____

_____

_____

_____

_____

_____

_____

_____

IDENTITY

Identity is defined as "the fact of being who or what a person or thing is." It refers to the qualities, beliefs, etc., that distinguish or identify a person or thing. It is the sense of who something, someone, or oneself is, or the recurring characteristics that enable the recognition of such an individual or group by others or themselves.

1. Read Jeremiah 1:5. Write down what this scripture means to you concerning your identity.

_____

_____

_____

_____

_____

_____

_____

2. Can you identify yourself simply as a son or daughter of the King? What does this identity look like? How well do you play your role? What are the challenges of seeing yourself as a son or daughter?

_____

_____

_____

_____

_____

_____

3. Looking at your current social groups or social connections. Do these groups align with who you currently are or are they representative of a former version of yourself? Explain.

_____

_____

_____

_____

_____

_____

_____

_____

THE ID, EGO, SUPEREGO

1. Is your current identity being influenced by the ID? How do you see its influence and control in your life?

_____

_____

_____

_____

_____

_____

_____

2. Is your current identity influenced by the ego? How do you see its influence and control in your life?

_____

_____

_____

_____

_____

_____

_____

3. Is your current identity influenced by the superego? How do you see its influence and control in your life?

_____

_____

_____

_____

_____

_____

_____

_____

4. How has suffering a loss affected or altered your personality?

_____

_____

_____

_____

_____

_____

_____

5. Have you experienced an "empty nest"? Did this transition come with grief? What emotions did you experience? What were the challenges of the transition? How did you process what you were feeling? How do you feel about it now? How did you reconcile this transition in your heart?

_____

_____

_____

_____

_____

_____

_____

_____

9
SAYING GOODBYE TO YESTERDAY

WHEN WHAT WAS CEASES TO BE

There are times when goodbye is a gesture of parting but in other situations that same goodbye could be in response to what remains after suffering a loss.

1. When the situation allowed you to, did having the opportunity to say goodbye make the loss less painful? Why? Why not? Did saying goodbye provide a sense of closure?

_____

_____

_____

_____

_____

_____

2. How have you come to terms with what has now ceased to be?

_____

_____

_____

_____

_____

_____

_____

TRIGGERED

Triggered is defined as a response caused by a particular action, process, or situation. Look at each of the below scenarios. Discuss how the scenario has impacted you, what emotions are still connected, what triggers you about the situation, how your triggers affect others, and ways that you have responded negatively. Also, identify positive coping strategies.

1. Death of a Loved One:

_____

_____

_____

_____

_____

_____

_____

2. End of a Relationship:

_____

_____

_____

_____

_____

_____

_____

3. Loss of Identity or Role:

_____

_____

_____

_____

_____

_____

_____

4. Loss of Health/Loss of Independence:

_____

_____

_____

_____

_____

_____

_____

5. Miscarriage, Stillbirth, or Abortion:

_____

_____

_____

_____

_____

_____

_____

6. Loss of a Home or Property:

_____

_____

_____

_____

_____

_____

_____

_____

7. Loss of Dreams and Expectations:

_____

_____

_____

_____

_____

_____

_____

_____

8. Loss of a Pet:

_____

_____

_____

_____

_____

_____

_____

_____

_____

9. Loss of Safety and Security:

_____

_____

_____

_____

_____

_____

_____

10.   Loss of Culture or Community:

_____

_____

_____

_____

_____

---

11.   Loss of Childhood:

10

THE ROAD LESS TRAVELED

JOURNEY TO HEALING

Inner healing is a form of emotional and spiritual therapy aimed at addressing and healing psychological wounds and traumas. This practice often focuses on identifying and resolving past hurts and negative experiences that affect an individual's current emotional well-being and behavior. The goal is to achieve emotional freedom, personal growth, and a sense of peace.

1. When you consider your journey to inner healing, where do you feel you are in the process? Have you avoided the journey because of the emotional pain? Have you started the journey but then stopped due to life? Have you addressed your wounds and are well on the path to healing?

_____

_____

_____

_____

_____

_____

_____

_____

2. What does emotional freedom mean to you? What emotions do you feel are a form of bondage? How will you know when you have acquired freedom in your emotions?

_____

_____

_____

_____

_____

_____

_____

_____

_____

_____

3. How do you define personal growth? What have been barriers or challenges to personal growth? How will you know when you have grown as a person?

_____

_____

_____

_____

_____

_____

_____

4. How do you define peace? Do you currently feel you are in a state of peace? If not, why? How will you know when you are at peace?

_____

_____

_____

_____

_____

_____

_____

_____

_____

_____

PRIORITIZING YOU

The truth is your healing may require a level of selfishness. Selfishness, in this regard, simply means that you are choosing to put "you" first.

1. When was the last time you made yourself a priority? What did you do? How did you feel? What prevents you from prioritizing yourself consistently?

_____

_____

_____

_____

_____

_____

_____

_____

2. Do you use being busy as a coping skill to avoid dealing with emotional pain? What does that look like to you? What emotions are you avoiding?

_____

_____

_____

_____

_____

_____

_____

_____

_____

_____

_____

_____

_____

LETTING GO

Merriam-Webster defines process as, "a series of actions or steps taken to achieve a particular end."

Consider the identified phases in "letting go." For each phase, write an action plan that identifies the steps you will take. Be sure to identify possible barriers and how you will overcome them. Bonus: include scriptures as a part of your action/battle plan.

1. Deciding to Let Go:

_____

_____

_____

_____

_____

_____

_____

_____

2. Acknowledging the Loss:

_____

_____

_____

_____

_____

_____

_____

_____

_____

_____

3. Embracing the Emotions:

_____

_____

_____

_____

_____

_____

_____

_____

_____

4. Honoring Memories:

_____

_____

_____

_____

_____

_____

_____

_____

_____

_____

5. Adapting to Change:

_____

_____

_____

_____

_____

_____

_____

_____

_____

6. Releasing Attachments:

_____

_____

_____

_____

_____

_____

_____

_____

_____

7. Seeking Support from Friends and Family:

_____

_____

_____

_____

_____

_____

_____

_____

_____

8. Permission to Heal:

_____

_____

_____

_____

_____

_____

_____

_____

_____

9. Respecting Timelines:

_____

_____

_____

_____

_____

_____

_____

_____

_____

_____

_____

_____

_____

_____

REFLECTIONS

REFLECTIONS

REFLECTIONS

Reflections

REFLECTIONS

REFLECTIONS

REFLECTIONS

REFLECTIONS

REFLECTIONS

REFLECTIONS

REFLECTIONS

REFLECTIONS

REFLECTIONS

REFLECTIONS

Made in the USA
Middletown, DE
25 August 2024

59139040R00066